JUST

Gigi

JUST Gigi

The Story of Gigi Catherine Rosselli

SUSAN BAIRD

Edited by Carol DeMare and Jill Cooley.

Book design by Jessika Hazelton
The Troy Book Makers • Troy, New York • thetroybookmakers.com
Printed in the United States of America

To order additional copies of this title,
contact your favorite local bookstore
or visit www.shoptbmbooks.com

ISBN: 978-1-61468-482-4

What good is sitting
alone in your room?
Come hear the music play.

Lines from the Song Cabaret

Gigi heard the music,
Danced to it,
Loved it.....
And lived her life to its beat.

CONTENTS

FOREWORD

Gigi Conboy Rosselli was my wife and the love of my life. It is hard for me to remember a time when we weren't together and I didn't love her. Her last few years on earth were both joyous and difficult. I know I wouldn't have survived without my faith. God kept me going when I thought I couldn't face another day. God also gave me earth angels to support and help me every day. These include our dear friend, Laura Szesnat, my sister, Barbara Rosselli and Gigi's niece, Mary Ellen Jeavons. They provided smiles, love and encouragement. I will be forever grateful.

Gigi always wanted her story told and here it is. She worked very hard on the beginning sections. When she became ill, I asked Gigi's cousin, Sue Baird, to finish it. The completed book is a tribute to her. I know you will love reading it as much as we enjoyed living it.

With Love,
Tom Rosselli

INTRODUCTION

Gigi Rosselli was my cousin, once removed. She and my mother were first cousins but we knew each other better because we were closer in age. In 2014, Gigi asked me to write her story in her voice. She had strong opinions about how it was to be worded and presented. She said she was never a victim and wanted the truth and only the truth told in the book.

The original story was never finished for reasons that you will learn as you read along. Gigi was brave, funny, smart and a pioneer in the local LGBT movement. Born a boy, she always knew she was a girl and never had any doubt in this conviction, even when everyone else said she was crazy. She started her own hair salon over 40 years ago and ran it with a generous nature and a lot of heart. She was always saying come over and I will give you a free cut, color, or anything you want. She loved people and would tell you that she loved you almost immediately after you met. And she meant it. In her business, she and her partner became the face of gay men in their community. It was and is a positive image.

Gigi and I didn't know each other well when growing up. But, I remember her father vividly. He was my grandmother's brother and, like Gigi, had a big personality and presence. The few times I saw the younger Gigi, who was then my second cousin George, he was quiet and withdrawn. I was shy and we would just stare each other down.

Neither of us made any effort to get to know the other better. After school, we both went our own ways. It wasn't until I was in my forties and one of my aunts became close with Gigi and her husband, Tom that I got to really know them. Gigi discovered that I wrote a book about our family's history in Cohoes (*Our House by the Falls*). She was excited about it and so proud of our shared family history. We talked about it for hours. She woke Tom in the middle of one night with the idea that I should write her story so that family, friends and the world in general could understand her journey. She also thought that the story could help others facing the same issues. We all thought it was a good idea and the project began.

The variation in the use of pronouns is difficult to follow but it can't be avoided. I use the pronoun her and then him and then back again. I try to make it match with who she was at that point. But, no matter what, George was always Gigi. They are one and the same. It was Gigi that I knew and loved so. She was quite a lady right up to the end. I know you will enjoy reading her story.

THE BEGINNING

Gigi was born on April 5, 1951 and named George John Conboy. His parents rejoiced at the arrival of a son and named him George for his grandfather and uncle, and John for his father (John Harold was his Dad's name). George was called many other names though: some nice and some awful. The youngest of six children, he came from a rowdy Irish family that was well known in the small town where they lived.

His grandmother ran a still in her basement during prohibition and one of his aunts reportedly dated one of his grandmother's best customers, Legs Diamond. Diamond was a notorious criminal of the Roaring Twenties. The brew made in the family home was said to be the best in the area. Afterwards, she modified the equipment to can fruit and vegetables and make chili sauce. She was a very resourceful and domestic woman. Family history says that her grandmother was never arrested for this slight violation of the law.

Everyone in the town knew and loved Gigi's father. He was known as Sparky because of the line work he did for the local power company. Gigi grew up in Cohoes and met her life partner nearby. They were together for over 40 years and for over 40 years ran successful businesses close to this same town. So, what is unusual? Well, first, at an early age, George realized that "he" was a "she" and as he got older he was attracted to boys, not girls. Then, he was a transgender male, frequently dressing as a woman. And, in his mid-60s he became who he was supposed to be all along, going from George to Butchie, to Georgie and finally to Gigi. This journey took years of hormone therapy, surgeries, counseling and personal torments. But, George became Gigi and this is her story.

BACKGROUND

Gigi was from small town America, born and raised in Cohoes, New York. Cohoes, ten miles north of the state's capital, Albany, was well known for its textile mills in the late 1800s and early 1900s. The population of the city surged in the 1800s with immigrants coming to work on the building of the mills; most then stayed to work in the mills they built. Her Irish ancestors came in the 1850s for this purpose. Almost all of the residents of the city were and are white and Catholic.

The immigrants from one country would settle in one area and build a church for their community. Consequently, there were two Irish churches, a Polish church, three French churches, an Italian church, a Ukrainian church and a Russian Orthodox Church. For Cohoes, this was cultural and ethnic diversity. The city was known for having a church on every corner. George's grandmothers and aunts frequented many of them, lighting candles to ask for the salvation of everyone's souls. Everyone very much needed their prayers. George's family went to St. Joseph's in the downtown area. Like his mother's family, the congregation was French Canadian.

Extensive housing was built for the mill workers; the buildings were brick, multi-family row houses. Many of the rest of the houses were two family flats. It was and is the type of community where everyone knows everyone. Housewives did their laundry on Monday mornings and gossiped over the clotheslines or got together at church socials to share news and talk about city activities. Most married their high school sweetheart and stayed married to the same person all of their lives. In many parts of the city, the immigrants' native languages were spoken at home and on the streets. After the mills closed and the textile industry moved south, the housing remained. If someone told you they were from Cohoes, the first thing you asked was from which part of the city. This was a community where most people looked and acted alike, but, ethnic distinctions were strong and remain to this day.

George's mother was Dorothy Trudeau, the daughter of Helena and Horace Trudeau who lived on the south side of the city. They had immigrated to Cohoes from Quebec in the late 1800s. Horace worked as a laborer in Cohoes when he could find jobs. When he couldn't, he'd hop (as in jump on) a train to go to one of the nearby communities to find work to support his family. But, sometimes he would have to go farther than Troy and he would be gone for six or seven months, sending money home. One of George's aunts ended up in the Poughkeepsie State Hospital for severe mental issues. Their entire family would go to visit her on Sundays; these visits were among George's earliest and scariest memories. People would be screaming and acting out and he would try to stay invisible and cling to his mother or father.

His father, John Harold Conboy, was the second youngest of the ten children of George and Mary Conboy, both children of Irish immigrants. They ran a store, inn, and tavern on the northern end of Cohoes on the Erie Canal. After the Canal closed, the house was moved to a spot overlooking the Cohoes Falls, one of the largest waterfalls in the state. Harold, Gigi's dad, was the favorite of his mother and was doted on by his two older sisters. They were old enough to be his mother. In his early twenties, he traveled with a vaudeville trope and saw a completely different way of life than what Cohoes provided. He was a roundabout and helped set up and tear down the show. He knew all the performers and was frequently their confidant. After he came home, he went to work for the local utility company and became a lineman. His mother was so against this since his older brother, George, had died doing this job in 1910. But, Harold fearlessly dealt with live wires and more than earned the nickname Sparky.

By the time he was 40, Harold developed a drinking problem that would plague him for the rest of his life. He was a friendly drunk and knew the local police force well. But, occasionally, someone else would pick him up and he would end up at "the university" for a while. When Harold said he was at the university for a bit, everyone knew he meant jail. Also, at times, the police would have him spend a night or two in jail so George's mother wouldn't kill him. Harold would come home drunk and without any money and Dorothy would physically attack him. Family, especially his cousin Stan would meet Harold at Danny's, a local bar and restaurant. Stan would slip Sparky some cash that they knew he used for drinks. Dorothy never knew about this while she struggled to pay the family's bills. George's grandmother had wanted Harold to take over the family home once she and his father died. But, because of his drinking problem, Harold's older brothers decided the home should go to one of his older sisters. George's mother, who desperately wanted to move "to the hill", never forgave Harold for this and Dorothy Conboy never stepped into the Conboy family home again.

George's family moved frequently, to different locations in Cohoes and once to Green Island. Living on Schuyler Street, Main Street, and Columbia Street, and later on North Mohawk Street, gave them identification with all the different areas of Cohoes. In each area, there were little neighborhood stores where people would congregate and visit. These were much like the little bodegas in New York City. George became close with the owners of Fisher's, Zullo's and Reevey's. They supported him through some difficult times. And, in Green Island, Annie Lazzaro and George became lifelong friends. These individuals were important to his life, giving him the support and sense of family that he didn't get at home. His father died in 1971 and his mom in 1986. George arranged to have his mother buried in St. Mary's Cemetery in Waterford where many members of the Conboy family rest.

When his father died, he was buried in a potter's field. No one knows why this happened. If any of his brothers and sisters had been alive they would have had buried him in St. Mary's Cemetery, but no one else did. It took George years to find his grave and have him moved to the family cemetery in Waterford. His first credit line was established by paying for Harold's gravestone; they called this the "book of the month". George had a payment book and mailed a coupon in with his payment for three years to pay for the stone, but pay for it he did. This is something that you should know about George and then Gigi: he and then she didn't give up. He looked for his father until he found him. He didn't have his parents buried together though. They hadn't lived together for years before their deaths and his father had specifically asked that he not be buried with Dorothy. He didn't want her talking about the family home and haunting him forever more. In a strange way, George said his parents really loved each other. But, they annoyed each other so much that they couldn't be together for a long period of time without wanting to kill each other.

George Conboy was born and raised, and eventually ran a hair salon near Cohoes. He never hid who he was and was open to discussing issues surrounding being gay and the transgender life. He didn't flaunt it but didn't deny it either. When he was young, he was made fun of and sometimes chased and beaten by those not understanding. But he was also encouraged to be himself and accepted by many. In this way, he was fortunate and he dearly loved all the people who helped him find his way. Gigi wanted this book dedicated with her love to all of them.

GEORGE

Dorothy Trudeau had two sons (Ed and Alan) from her first marriage to Charles Macey. After Charles died, she met and married John Harold Conboy. They had four more children, Mary, Shirley, and Diane, and their one son George. Life in their house was chaotic and, at times, difficult. First, it was crowded, with everyone living in small spaces. When George's mother and father married, Dorothy thought that since Harold's family seemed to have money, he did too. They both had very different expectations of what marriage would bring.

Harold, who didn't have money, developed a drinking problem and frequently fought with his wife. Alcohol consumed much of his income. George's mother had hereditary depression and frequently emotionally and mentally, was not there for any of her children. The problem went untreated throughout her life. George loved them both but did not get much support, guidance or love from them in return. His older siblings were forced to stand in for his parents: but they didn't want this role. As a result, George received very little parental attention, love or affection.

In an effort to be the son his father wanted, George played little league in grade school. He played left and right fields and frequently someone would tell him that he threw like a girl. He did. The best part of those nights was that he would sit on the porch of one of his father's brothers on Vliet Street, either before or after the game.

His aunt and uncle were so kind and so normal that he loved just being there. They would give him ice cream and just let him sit with them and enjoy the summer nights. It felt so safe, something that he rarely felt at home. His Aunt Rita and Uncle Frank paid attention to him and listened when he talked. The environment there was peaceful. He yearned for a life like this. He so wanted love and acceptance, and normalcy.

George first realized that he was different from the other boys in third grade. He didn't like the games that the neighborhood boys played. They wanted to be baseball players or astronauts when they grew up. He wanted to be a girl. Actually, he believed that he was already a she. But, he kept quiet about his beliefs and ambitions. He would quietly "borrow" his mother's clothes and make up and go to the basement to play dress up. His mother knew but never said anything, but his sisters would yell and tell him to take the clothes off and go outside and play with the other boys. When he was 11, he got caught shop-lifting hair curlers and hair products from a local five and dime. The family got him out of trouble but at home no one talked about this or any of his other activities. He was already very interested in how his hair and face looked and how he walked and behaved. Someone told me he would "parade" up and down Congress Street perfecting his walk. He was usually alone and seemed isolated from the other children.

As he grew, some teachers encouraged him to be true to himself no matter what. Ms. English, a well-known teacher, would have him dance for the class and encouraged him to perform. Ms. Curtin told him to be true to himself. Others though would make fun of him, sometimes without his knowing. For example, when he was 12 or 13, he would buy flowing flowered tops to wear with his bell bottoms to a local canteen on the weekends. When he wore them to school, one teacher would ask him to model them across the front of the room. Much later, he found out that the teacher was mocking him with his male students. At a local Canteen at St. Agnes Church, girls loved to dance with George because he danced so well. Once he won a trophy and some of the boys waited outside and beat him with the trophy that he was so proud of. Sadly, the beating was part of the prize and was remembered more than the trophy. On another night, he tried to bleach his short dark hair and turned it the color of a yellow-orange onion. Proud as ever, he used gel to spike it and went to the canteen completely at ease with the odd-colored hair. He was a definite trend setter. Years later, both Ms. English and Ms. Curtin would come to his salon on Fulton Street in Troy to get their hair done. George loved them both and they were proud of the George they nurtured.

By middle school, George had several friends who would protect him no matter what the situation. He thought that the leader of Butchie's (that is what they called George) gang was also gay. It was with him in the old soap factory on Central Avenue in Cohoes that George shared his first kiss. He had his first awkward sexual experience with another member of this group in the same place. The three of them never talked about this and went on as guy friends. Once he got to be 15 or 16, he was very open about who he was. On Saturday nights, he would dress up in his mother's clothes and walk up and down Remsen Street, Cohoes' main street. Gigi later said that this was George's coming out. (Gigi frequently spoke like George was another person and one that she didn't like very much. She was not only emotionally distant from the memories, but spoke about them like they were someone else's past not hers). Frequently, one of his half-brothers would find him and yell for him to get in the car before someone killed him. If no one else did, the embarrassed family vowed to kill him themselves.

Once, right in front of City Hall, Alan pulled up and told George to stop wearing their mother's dresses because he was a boy. George responded by calmly telling him that he was a girl and kept walking proud. He was so certain of this. Years later, Alan visited Gigi and asked to go through her closet with her. He then told her he was happy that she was who she was supposed to be. This was shortly before Alan passed away and just a few years before Gigi became ill. By then, both Gigi and Alan were at peace with their relationship and respected the other as they were

Sometimes other kids chased George, but he had several hiding spots that were very small. He could get in but the other boys couldn't. Gigi later talked about how good George felt during these walks on Remsen Street and was in no way sorry for them. But, she also talked about how afraid he was when a group would chase him. Other guys would make obscene gestures and call George names, but the worst was the group harassment that he frequently faced. He wanted to belong while remaining true to himself and this just wasn't possible. The support he felt from some was offset by the harassment he received from others.

George also had several friends who were girls. He and his friend, Debbie Dumas, would cut classes at Cohoes High School and go to Debbie's house and fool with makeup and hair all day. Debbie later said that her friends knew that George was gay but they never talked about it with each other or with him. They just enjoyed their friendship. George enjoyed those times so much and remembered them vividly. Thank goodness Mr. Dumas never discovered them. Those who knew him said that he would have not seen them as two girls having fun.

George told his father that he was gay when he was 17. It wasn't a difficult conversation since Harold was fairly worldly from his vaudeville days. There were also many clues to George's gender identity. They sat on their porch on Columbia Street and talked about it for a long time. Harold wasn't shocked but was worried. He said that it was a difficult life and that George should always be careful about sharing the details of his life with others. George also told his mother he was gay but Dorothy just said that she was glad, and that she wanted George to be happy. When he said that wasn't what he meant, his mother walked out of the room. Dorothy was so naive and unaware that it just didn't register what being gay meant. By this time, the term was openly used to define homosexuals. Dorothy didn't realize this though. Many knew that George was gay, but no one ever brought the subject up. It was the elephant in the room that they never talked about. But, Gigi still remembered many of her friends for their kind hearts and acceptance.

George graduated from high school shortly after his 17th birthday. The Vietnam War was in full swing and most boys immediately received a draft notice. He did too. George didn't know how else to tell them who he was, so he dressed up in some of his mother's best and went for the interview. There was one other person dressed the same way. He said that they both looked like Corporal Klinger on MASH. Both were quickly sent upstairs to the psych unit. George received a deferment but not due to psychological problems. The doctor thought he was sane but undergoing an identity crisis that would not be tolerated in service. Without any other employment opportunities, George went to work for the public employment program (CETA) in Cohoes. There, he was lucky to be taken under the wings of a few prominent politicians and city leaders. As he was able to support himself, he moved out of his parents' home. He found the quiet and peace of living alone wonderful, but, it also gave him time to dwell on some issues that were not resolved.

Years later, when she talked about these events, Gigi was very matter-of-fact and calm. No emotion at all. She said that she was always comfortable with who she was. But, it was clear that some of these events had scarred her at deep levels. And, then, there was religion. She didn't go to Catholic schools but regularly attended religious education. She learned that it was a mortal sin to be homosexual. Those feelings remained with her throughout her life as a man and would surface at unexpected times. Secondly, the beatings and the alienation from many of her peers left feelings of isolation and depression that would surface later. The only direct conversation that she had with anyone about being gay was when she came out to her father. This she remembered as a beautiful moment. She believed she was a woman and always acted that way. Surprisingly, the Cohoes community was mostly accepting of this. At the same time, Gigi realized that many saw her as strange. She knew that she was the subject of ridicule and shame from some of her neighbors and even friends. She was different, alone and uncertain about her future, and she really didn't have anyone in her life to talk to about this. She just held her chin high and went forward any way she could.

THE MEAN QUEEN

When he started with CETA, George worked at the main library in Cohoes. Mostly, he sat in the basement, cataloging and checking books in. After a while, some of the other workers started teasing and bullying him and the supervisors moved him to a library annex on Berkley Avenue. Over time, he started doing the hair of most of his coworkers and supervisors. He had a little routine, greeting guests with something to drink, washing their hair in his kitchen sink and cutting hair while the customer sat on a kitchen chair. He called it the Kitchen Salon. George had a real gift for styling and charged only $5 for a cut. He was so happy and thought that he was getting rich from the income. Actually, he was able to buy clothes for entertaining at the local gay clubs with this added income. By then, he had his first apartment on Cataract Street in one of the old mill houses. It was small, dingy and dark. He loved it. Later, he moved to a bigger apartment on 144 Remsen Street over a small store, Kenney Curtains.

At times, CETA would send him out to help older residents. One lady asked him to clean her toaster. So, George dutifully put it in a pan of soapy water and washed it. This wasn't what the woman meant. It didn't work after this and the cost was deducted from his pay. It was about this time that he started to go to the gay clubs in the area and eventually to the ones in New York

City. He discovered a passion for dressing up as a woman and doing imitations of his heroines, Liza Minnelli, Cher and Barbra Streisand. It was like strutting up and down Remsen Street, only so much better.

Saturdays were spent roaming stores looking for bargains on slinky clothes for the act, and then on Saturday night, he would walk or take the bus to one of the local clubs such as the old Dave Denny Barn in Colonie or the Shangri La in Menands. He met other crossdressers that performed in the same clubs and they frequently went shopping and to the clubs together. One friend continually asked George to borrow clothes and makeup, and then wanted to perform to George's songs. George would always say "No". The friend started calling George "one mean queen". The nickname stuck and George was widely known as "The Mean Queen". He liked it and thought it meant that he was fiercely protective of not only his things but also his friends. He was determined to stay true to himself and the woman that was inside. A mean queen he was and would stay. When entertaining, George used the name Cathy of Cohoes. No one at the bars ever heard the name George Conboy. He liked Cathy a lot and hid in her persona at the bars and clubs.

At the Shangri La, the owners, Marge and Frenchie, took a liking to George and helped him develop an act. On nice summer nights, he would find a ride to Mr. Chips in Lake George. Once, the owner there told George he was winning the night's prize for best performance for his imitation of Cher, who he was dressed as. The owner then went into the restroom and George sat on a bench waiting for him. He never came back. Turned out, he had a major heart attack and died.

George became so hysterical that everyone thought he was the man's wife. But, he was very upset that he wouldn't be getting the night's trophy. The prizes and recognition were very important. Recognition of any sort seemed like acceptance and George would always work for and crave this.

NEW YORK, NEW YORK

After World War II, there were efforts to bring everything back to the prewar normal. Everyone was supposed to conform. George grew up in this environment but didn't conform and desperately looked for a place where he felt he belonged. While he was mostly accepted in Cohoes, this was because his family was well known and he was viewed as eccentric and funny. For Cohoes, the postwar era brought new housing, with the development of single-family homes on one side of the hill and larger residences for the more affluent on the other side. The smaller homes were built by veterans through a program sponsored by the federal government. Many of the veterans bought the homes at reduced costs and interest rates. While Cohoes was developing its residence patterns, in San Francisco and New York City, there were underground gay clubs and communities. The big cities offered a more exciting environment for someone like George who felt out of place in Cohoes and wanted to belong somewhere.

By the time, he was 18, George was a favorite performer at the local gay clubs. He looked natural when dressed as a woman. He was not a drag queen. He would sit seductively on the piano and sing Cher and Judy Garland songs and receive a lot of applause. Several bar patrons had told him that he was wasting his time in Albany and that he could be very successful in a bigger city. So a natural progression from local performances seemed to be going to New York

City. After working for CETA for about a year, the eighteen year old George and a friend took a bus to New York City and their adventure began. George and his friend, Joey, became part of the gay community in New York City.

At that time in New York City, there were two distinct centers for homosexual men: the area around Times Square or downtown. At first, George and his friend lived in an area near Times Square. George quickly wanted to get away from this neighborhood though. Most were hustlers and lived by selling themselves on the Street. He wouldn't do this and decided to go downtown. His friend stayed uptown and hustled for a living.

In 1969, you were not supposed to be openly gay in New York City. If you walked the streets holding hands with someone of the same sex, the police would stop you and arrest you if you refused to stop the hand holding. In June of 1969, during a raid at the Stonewall Club, a gay club on Christopher Street in Greenwich Village, the patrons spontaneously protested the arrests and a movement began. Gays were saying enough of keeping our identities "in the closet". We can be who we are. After Stonewall, gays and lesbians began the fight for equality and to establish their own communities. George was in the City and was part of the protests. He was by no means a leader and not vocal about the cause. But, he was a body that went along with the group and added numbers to the cause. In August, someone asked George to go to a music festival with him in the Catskills. George said yes; he was thinking hotels, regular meals and a hot shower. When he got to Woodstock, he was appalled and said it was worse than living on the street in the city. He hitchhiked back to the City and never saw that man again. But, as so many others, what he really wanted was to make it big in the entertainment world. He spent the majority of a year trying to make a place for himself in the big Apple, performing in clubs wherever he could.

New York was both exhilarating and scary. Sometimes he had shelter and food and sometimes he didn't. His father taught him to be street smart and wise. Otherwise, he probably would have been hurt or killed. He was a "Go-Go Boy" and performed in clubs like Stonewall, the Baths in the old Ansonia Hotel, Peter and the Rabbit, the Pink Pussy Owl, Bon Soiree and Orange Julius. When presented with the opportunity, he would dress up and dance in the elevated cages and look for success in entertaining. It just never came. But, he saw many up and coming celebrities perform especially at the Baths. One night, a young woman performed; she was very outgoing and raunchy. George thought she would never make it. But, Bette Midler proved him wrong. Her piano player, a man named Barry Manilow, who was wrapped in a towel at the piano, also did okay for himself. Bette Midler would later state that she took pride in her performances at the gay bathhouses and felt she was at the forefront of the Gay Liberation Movement.

In addition to the club scene, George made money wherever he could. The bead lady of lower Manhattan would give him food and money to do errands for her and run her stand when she was not there. Her motto was "Bells and Beads and All Your Needs, Come to Momma Hippie". She was very eccentric but George really liked her and enjoyed working for her. He also ran errands for Carnegie Deli in exchange for food. But, in the end, he knew he couldn't live there forever without a job and home, and he went back to Cohoes.

A haunting memory of this time is that he made many friends who later died of AIDS. He would always remember them and the fun that they had together and the tragedy of their early deaths. For many years, George and then Gigi would go to "The Night of the 1,000 Gowns" in New York City, dressing up and entertaining. This is a major fundraiser for AIDS programs and is attended by many celebrities. Years later, Mayor Rudy Giuliani expanded the event to help the homeless. He was working to provide homes for those that lived on the streets in Times Square, many of whom were also gay. George performed at this event in memory of the gay and transgender individuals he met in the city and who later died from AIDS.

Everyone said that George had a difficult childhood. But he was always smiling and stylish, even as a child. Love the bow tie and the hat
in the picture with his mother and Tootie. The second picture shows
George learning to dance with Tootie in the family's living room.

George sitting in his family's living room in one of his beloved flowered shirts. His eyes look so sad.

George with a few friends in his mid-teens. This is when they started going to gay clubs in the Albany Area.

George dressed for entertaining on one of the swings at the clubs in New York City.

An ad in the Troy paper. In his early days as a stylist, George would place ads to tell his customers of his new location. He developed a loyal customer base that went with him and stayed with him when he bought his own salon.

This was taken at the Salon on Fulton Street in Troy. George and Tom with two of their employees and a customer.

An early picture of George and Tom.

George and Tom at a wedding in Saratoga. They were always the life of the party; a fun couple and so good looking.

George with Marge Conboy. Calling them "The Boys", she became very friendly with the couple and was the link that connected many of the Conboy family to them.

George with his niece Mary Ellen and two of his great-nieces. He loved children and was a beloved Uncle George to many. When he became Aunt Gigi, they all accepted the change. For a while though, many still called her Uncle George.

George with Tootie, Alan and Ed. The hair was starting to grow out here. The transition had begun.

George with his niece, Theresa Thibodeau, her mother Jean, and George's Aunt, Jeannie Thibodeau. He was thinner and his facial features had softened here. Another step in transition.

VISITING THE DARK PLACES

During the years in Cohoes and the time in New York City, the opportunity for drinking and experimenting with drugs was everywhere. George's father suffered from alcoholism and his mother had severe depression. His mother was emotionally distant unless she was encouraging her children to do something wrong. George's sister worked for a local grocery store where part of her job was letting the owner feel and touch her. She begged her mother to let her quit. Dorothy just said that she was exaggerating and that she had to continue with her job. In truth, they badly needed the money but being abused was beyond what they wanted to accept. Seeking solace in liquor and depression seemed natural for all of them.

Eventually, George admitted that he came from a very dysfunctional home. His parents were not happy and neither spent a lot of time raising and caring for their children. His father was a good dad when he tried, but he was more attached to his drinking and her mother just lived in her own world. Harold would come home after drinking all of his pay and Dorothy would physically attack him. Everyone stayed out of their way. George didn't blame them although maybe he should have. He moved out of their home as soon as he could and started the life he wanted to lead. He was always running away from the life he lived as a child and was determined to build a better life for himself.

With all the clubbing, George's drinking was out of control. It dulled the pain and isolation that he felt. He would go to work hungover and sometimes very drunk. He was late and missed a lot of time. But, the worst was when he went in hungover. He was loud and very funny, and very disruptive. Or, he could be mean and disruptive. The destructive behavior spread to his private life. He would get depressed and call his friends in the middle of the night telling them he was going to kill himself. He was not depressed about being gay but rather depressed about being considered such an oddity. He felt that people should just accept him as he was. During this period, he set his apartment on fire in an apparent suicide attempt. He was arrested but not offered help, and the judge agreed to dismiss the charges if he stayed out of trouble for six months. On another night, he and a group of his crossdressing friends walked down the middle of a street in Albany. All were drunk and carried open cans of beer, despite an open container law. They dared the police to arrest them, which of course they did. Once in jail, George became hysterical because of being "locked up". He begged to be released but the officers told him the only way he could get out was if his tears melted the bars. So stay he did. He was really a child looking for attention and assurance that everything would be okay. He didn't receive any counseling and continued to spiral out of control.

The administrators at the Cohoes CETA program watched the deterioration and tried to help. Today, this would have been called an intervention. They persuaded George to go to the St. Peter's Rehab program in Albany. There, the administrator tried desperately to help. The outpatient rehab would help for a while and then the drugs and drinking pattern would return. This went on for a few years until everyone (except maybe George) thought he needed inpatient care. His CETA friends came through with a 30-day scholarship to a nationally known rehabilitation center in Pennsylvania. Even the round trip plane fare was paid in advance. This gift turned George's life around and shows what an amazing community he lived in. They not only accepted him, they helped in any way they could.

The early days at rehab were terrifying. The center was situated on several hundred acres in the middle of nowhere. Most of the residents were older men, but the facility was in the process of reaching out to younger addicts like George. He was in his early twenties and it was scary, both the place and process. He was still withdrawing from drugs and alcohol and everything seemed intimidating, especially his roommate. He was an older man who stayed under the covers all day making strange noises and talking to himself. George was afraid to sleep because he thought he would be attacked at any minute. He spent a lot of time sitting in the activity room and crying. One day, a very nice woman asked if she could help. George told her he was afraid to go to his room and hadn't slept in days. The woman offered to take him to his room and sit with him while he slept. As it turned out, George's roommate was the woman's father and every time she visited their conversations would boost George's spirits. Later, George found out she was a television personality. George's talks with her helped a great deal and Gigi always wanted to thank her for taking the time to help a despondent young man who was really a woman.

The rest of the time in Pennsylvania was uneventful but difficult. First, there was the detox process. He went through it all: shaking, fear and nausea, always with an intense desire for a drink and pills. It seemed like it took forever to get everything out of his system. He walked down the driveway many times wanting to run away, but didn't. Someone would follow him and they would sit and talk and eventually George would go back. It was always his choice. No one forced him to do anything. He did the detox, intense counseling, exercise and group activities. Then, they told him that he was ready for release. Interestingly, they never talked to him about gender identification. They dealt with substance abuse only. When the topic of release was raised, the fear came back again, big time. Counselors strongly advised George not to go back to Cohoes where he would be exposed to his parents' dysfunction. They also told him to avoid all situations that would make him want a drink or reach for the pills. But, he didn't know where else to go. When he got off the plane in Albany, one of his sponsors was there waiting for him and assured him that everything would be all right. And, to his and everyone else's amazement, it really was.

Once home, he again went to work for CETA. He realized that he couldn't do this all of his life and decided to finish the beauty school classes that he started before he went to the residential rehab program. He had a real gift for cutting and setting hair. He knew that this should be his career goal. Also, the busier he was, the less temptation he faced with alcohol and drugs. His thinking had cleared enough to plan for the future. George dated many men during this time; he was even with one for a few years. This man was abusive and beat George when he was drunk. George thought he was really in love and held on for dear life. Later, he told George he was straight. He left George and married a woman; together they had five children.

George hadn't found the one that he was sure was for him. He didn't even know if he wanted to find someone. Then, on August 5, 1978, at the Eight Ball Club on Central Avenue in Albany, he met Thomas Rosselli. He didn't realize it then, but between a career and a new partner his life's path was set.

TOM

On the night that they met. Thomas Rosselli was 17 years old and still in high school. George Conboy was 26, out of rehab and struggling with sobriety. When he went to the clubs, he frequently slipped, and was more than a little intoxicated that night. Some friends from the salon where Tom washed hair snuck him into the club to listen to the music. Tom was the son of first generation Italian-Americans who lived in Albany. He lived in a house with extended family on each floor (aunts, grandparents) and had a completely different childhood than what George experienced. Each meal at their home was a feast with all the family present. And, there was always lots of laughter and love. He had done sports in school and attended all of the proms and school functions. He was a social butterfly; if something was going on, he was there. An altar boy, he was and still is a devout Catholic. The second youngest of four children, he had one older brother and two sisters. All went to Catholic schools. At 17, he hadn't had a serious romance but thought eventually he would meet someone and get married.

Tom was taking beauty school classes at night and was set to get his license to do hair at the same time that he graduated from high school the following spring. His uncle ran a salon in Albany and his grandfather was a barber. He came from a "hair" family and thought his future was set. The night they met, George asked if Tom wanted to go outside and have a smoke and Tom said he didn't smoke. Then, George asked him if he would like a drink and he said he didn't drink. Dancing was all that was left and Tom loved to dance. Afterwards, George was surprised and flattered that Tom pursued him. The day after they met Tom visited the bar to try to find George. He contacted George and they agreed to meet at the club again that Wednesday night. George didn't usually go out during the week to avoid the temptation of drinking. He was really trying to be sober. But, there was something about Tom. Both describe it as not just physical. There was an immediate connection that neither could ignore. They were together from that point on. Tom said that he didn't know whether he was gay or straight but when he saw George, he saw kind eyes and a beautiful heart that drew him in. He knew right away that he wanted to be with him.

There were all sorts of barriers to a relationship. George lived in Cohoes and Tom lived in Albany. The cities were 10 miles apart. Neither owned a car. To see each other, they had to take three buses; each way was at least an hour. Also, Tom's friends warned him that George drank too much and was a female impersonator. He just didn't care. His family, especially his mother, was very supportive and told him to follow his heart. His family was Mediterranean emotional, always voicing their feelings. When George met Tom's mother, Mrs. Rosselli opened her arms and welcomed him into her home and family. He finally knew what it was like to have a mother and a family. Tom's mother asked him what Cohoes was like and he responded that everyone was white and that there was no racial diversity. He had lived at 110 Grand Street in lower Albany, close to Lincoln Park, and was used to a multiracial culture. He couldn't understand how George had come from Cohoes and survived such a homogenous area while staying true to himself. George even said that he loved Cohoes and the people there. They were his family.

Gigi didn't want to give the impression that everything was always all right with Tom's family. One of Tom's beloved aunts refused to believe that he was gay and wanted to send him away to "save and cure him". His brother was also not supportive and wanted nothing to do with the relationship. He was upset about the age difference and George's past, including the drinking and drug use. So, Mama Josephine Rosselli had a sit down one week before Sunday dinner and told everyone that Tom and George were a couple and that everyone needed to support and respect them. Everyone may not have agreed, but they were silent from that point on. Gigi believed that the family hoped that Tom would be a priest, but that just wasn't to be.

A year later, after he finished high school and was 18, Tom moved in with Gigi and both started their careers as stylists. At first, they lived in Gigi's small apartment in downtown Cohoes. Later, they moved to a larger apartment on the hill and then bought a trailer in Halfmoon. This was followed by the purchase of three homes, each one a little larger. They stayed in the first two houses seven years each, and have owned their last home for 21 years. This path was so similar to the life progression of straight couples. With their jobs, they both started working at salons in local malls. Then, they started their own business in downtown Troy. They stayed on Fulton Street for 19 years and then moved to a larger location in Latham. Latham is a suburb of Albany and very close to Cohoes and Troy. The salon is still located there. They had a large, devoted client base and had a wonderful time visiting and joking with them. Many became family. They were always open and told everyone that they were a couple. They became role models and faces for gay couples to their many conservative customers.

To most of their customers, their sexual orientation didn't matter. This is surprising since Troy and Cohoes are small communities with old fashioned views and values. It was the same at home. Their life was pretty normal and they were very happy. They had a comfortable division of duties: Gigi did the business management of the salons and Tom did the scheduling and day to day workings. The salon also gave Gigi a platform to perform, which she and their customers loved. At home, Gigi took care of the housekeeping and Tom, who has an amazing green thumb, did the outside work. Tom, with his Italian heritage, is a wonderful cook and did the shopping and cooking. On many weekend afternoons, they would visit Washington Park in Albany. Here, many gays and transgender individuals gathered in nice weather. Tom and Gigi would bring their scissors and perform hair miracles on park benches. This was their community and they helped in any way they could.

No matter how good life was, there were still things that bothered George about himself. He knew that he would address these issues at some point. Inside George was sure he was a woman, but his body said something else. He knew that had to change. The question was when and what would Tom do when his longtime male partner became a woman.

Tom's grandparents who immigrated to the United States from Italy. After living in New York City, they moved to Albany.

A very young Tom sitting on the steps of the family home on Grand Street in Albany.

The four Rosselli children sitting on their family's sofa on Easter Sunday. From the left: Mary Jo, Sal, Tom and Barbara.

A few years later; Tom, Barbara and Mary Jo.

Tom's first Communion in 1967.

Christmas at the Rosselli's was always special and happy; this is Tom and Mary Jo holding their gigantic tootsie rolls and the dinner table set up in the living room to accommodate the crowd.

Tom's older brother Sal; the resemblance is striking.

Tom's high school graduation picture. Shortly after this, he and Gigi moved into together. They had been a couple for a year.

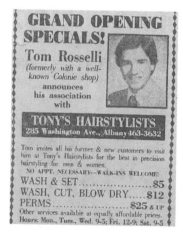

An ad announcing Tom's joining the staff at his uncle's salon in Albany.

Mrs. Rosselli and Tootie on the first Christmas that Tom and George were together. Mrs. R. always included Gigi's family in their gatherings. They all finally had a real family.

The entire Rosselli family on a summer outing.

Mrs. Rosselli's 75th Birthday party. Barbara is giving her a kiss, Sal is on the right and Mary Jo is between Sal and Mrs. R.

GIGI

Since childhood, George had told everyone that he was a girl. When his brothers said that he was a boy, he said no he was a girl. At the draft board and CETA, when psychiatrists said that he was having an identity crisis; he told them he was not and asked about surgery. The doctors would not even consider it, saying they could "cure him". And, then, life happened. George went to rehab, met Tom and they built a good life and business together. George grew into a handsome, confident man. His Irish heritage came through in a beautiful complexion and rosy cheeks. His mother's Franco-American genes came through in deep penetrating eyes and a little craziness. He would do the most outrageous things.

Throughout, he always thought about transition surgery; Tom knew this and participated in many discussions about "the" decision. Starting in his late forties, George would have a nip and tuck here and there to soften his features. First, there were hair transplants to shorten the forehead. Then, there was a tracheal shave to make the Adam's apple less prominent, a mini-facelift, cheek fillers, a forehead lift and corrective surgery to fix the eye problems created by the forehead lift. George even had his teeth capped to be more curved than male teeth. Most people don't know that there is a difference. Some of these procedures were so painful and resulted in weeks of recuperation. The suffering cannot be adequately described in words. George also had waxing, electrolysis and laser work done, removing all excess hair. Tom said he would sit in the waiting room and listen to the screams and he would cry. When he came out, George would smile and say he was fine. After each surgery, there would be doubts about whether to continue. And being brought up Catholic, he saw himself as being eternally damned. But, he did continue and truly became a "she". He just couldn't stop pursuing what he knew to be true.

George started to dress as a woman whenever he could. He took lessons to change the characteristics of and soften his voice. A big step was going to stores to look for women's clothes. In Chico's, he made a friend with a sales clerk named Carol and told her his story. He asked her help in selecting his first female wardrobe and to develop confidence in going to woman's stores to do his every day shopping. Carol eventually became a make-up consultant and helped George find makeup that looked natural with his coloring. Later, while shopping with one of his cousins, George tried on women's clothes. His cousin was speechless until she got home and recovered her voice enough to call other relatives to tell them what happened. They remained friends, but afterwards there was a distance that wasn't there before. With each procedure, he thought that maybe everything would be okay, but he never was satisfied and never felt whole.

National data shows that 3,240 transition surgeries were performed in 2016. Of this number, 1,759 or 54 percent were male to female (MTF). There are about 1.4 million transgender individuals in the United States, but not all will have gender-changing surgery. The majority of patients are in their 20s or early 30s and are single. The reason for the surgery is listed as Gender Identity Disorder or Gender Dysphoria. Early in the 1960s individuals in the United States had to go out of the country for this surgery, most frequently to Canada. Today, it is offered at many locations in the United States and there are national experts in the field at Johns Hopkins and Stanford. The most frequently used technique for the MTF procedure is known as penile inversion. The penis is split in two and inserted inside to make a vagina; the bladder is then rerouted and excess tissue is used to form a vulva.

When Gigi was ready, there was no surgeon in New York State that had approval to perform this surgery and they had to go out of State to find a provider. The approval process includes providing evidence of dressing and living as a woman, counseling, hormone therapy, letters of support from attending physicians and insurance approval. Of course, you also have to have the funds to pay for the uncovered expenses. The most important questions you need to answer are why do you want this surgery and why do you want it now. The process itself is not easy. During it, you have to deal with the changes in your body and the prejudices of the medical community and the people that you deal with every day. It takes years and there are many times that you want to give up. But, Gigi said that if you know you are really a woman, try as you may, you just can't give up. And she never did.

The answer for the first question was easy for her. Gigi had always felt that she was a woman and the steps that she had taken didn't satisfy her need for a complete transition. The "why now" question came down to "because she could". She was at a point in her business and home life where she could do it and Tom as always was completely supportive. Any fears of what the surgery would mean to their relationship were unspoken. They both knew that their love was strong enough to survive and whatever happened they would cope with the outcomes. Of course, there was doubt that was fed by their families and they both eventually admitted that they had fears themselves about what would happen.

After proving that you have dressed as a woman for at least a year (they had mounds of pictures and witnesses to confirm this), you start seeing a psychiatrist. For Gigi, this was the head psychiatrist at Albany Medical Center who had a specialty of treating sexual identity issues. At first, it was just Gigi who went to these appointments, and then Tom started accompanying her. When someone is in a serious relationship, the transition affects the partner as well as the patient.

After about a year of counseling, Gigi was referred to an endocrinologist at the Albany Medical Center. To prepare for surgery, she was put on a high dose of estradiol. The hormones affect and slowly change all of the soft tissues in your body. Tom was a saint during this process. Gigi would be manic some days and on other days had trouble getting out of bed. Tom just dealt, no matter who she was on any given day. She slowly grew small breasts, her body became very thin and her hips narrowed. She was starting to look more like a woman and she liked it and showed it off. It was at this point that many realized Gigi was really doing this. Gigi loves to make an entrance and would be intentionally late for appointments. George looked a lot like Paul McCartney with broader shoulders. Now, Gigi would walk into the salon, tall and proud, with long black hair, slim hips and shoulders and legs that went on forever. The first thing you noticed was how well she walked in high heels. The transition was amazing. It was summer and she would wear high platform shoes and white pants. She looked stunning. She was close to the final stages before the major surgery and loved showing off her new self. She was a "she" in all aspects except one.

Gigi and Tom partying in New York City. By the late 1990's, George had become Gigi and dressed as a woman all of the time. What a good looking couple they were.

Gigi entertaining. She loved the stage and never hesitated to take a microphone. The two pictures on the bottom are from the Night of 1,000 Gowns in New York City.

Gigi rehearsing an act at home early one morning. When preparing to perform, she would wake Tom up and tell him that something wasn't right with her act and up they would get up no matter the time.

Entertaining and working at the salon.

A favorite picture of Gigi and Tom.

Gigi dressed for a date with her guy before they were married.

Tom and Gigi with an old friend that stopped into the salon to say hello. They hadn't seen each other in 25 years when she stopped in to say hello, not realizing Gigi was ill. It was amazing that they reconnected with so many friends during this time.

By this time, George was using the name Gigi. Everyone thought that it was a shortened version of George. Gigi loved the movie "Gigi" and always had a sketch of Leslie Caron as Gigi in the salon. Gigi named herself for the character of Gigi, who in her mind epitomized femininity. Becoming Gigi was her goal. People would still call her George. But, she would calmly correct them and say "Just Call Me Gigi". When work was started on the book in 2014, this was going to be the title. But then it was used by someone else and the book's title was changed. Gigi was still well at this time and was not pleased.

The final step in the physician process was seeing an urologist at the Albany Center. This doctor had previously done transition surgeries in Albany and said he would have done the surgery himself if he could. But, there had been a 17-year ban on the surgery in New York State. After Governor Andrew Cuomo lifted the ban on May 1, 2015, he also required all insurance companies operating in the State to cover the procedure. But before this, the Doctor in Albany referred Gigi to Dr. Christine McGinn in New Hope, PA. All of the doctors gave letters of support to Dr. McGinn which formed a strong foundation for Gigi's request.

The last local step of the transition was getting approval from her insurance company. Tom handled most of the paperwork and climbing through the hoops. The big barrier was that there was no local surgeon who performed the surgery and they had to go out of network. Of course, prior approval was needed and they needed to deal with several case managers and had to be able to pay for the services not covered. National data suggests that on average a transition patient pays $20,000 to $30,000 out of pocket. Tom spoke with almost every employee at the HMO and even ended up speaking with the president of the HMO himself. Each plan and provider has its own requirements for approving such a surgery. Theirs included the physician letters, no smoking for the month prior to the surgery, a healthy Body Mass Index (BMI), stopping all hormone therapy two weeks before surgery, electrolysis and laser work of the surgical site (much more painful laser work) and paying a significant copayment. Gigi had stopped smoking a long time before this and easily complied with the other criteria. In addition, they both had to be able to stay two weeks post-surgery at Dr. McGinn's facility in Pennsylvania. Gigi, wanting to be as authentic as possible, had everything treated with a laser: her fingers, toes and stomach, back. Once again, Tom waited while two attendants held her down and she screamed. But, afterwards, they were ready for and terrified of the next steps.

TRANSITION

They finally had all the needed approvals, most importantly the one from Gigi's insurance company, to go out of network. She thought that they would be going to some large city. Instead, Dr. McGinn was at the Papillon Center in New Hope, PA. The Center and Dr. McGinn are nationally known for their work with transition surgeries. Dr. McGinn has appeared on several national programs, including the Oprah Show and Dr. Oz. She was also featured in the documentary "Trans", released in 2012. She has brought visibility and positive publicity to the transition process. New Hope is on the Delaware River about halfway between New York City and Philadelphia. It is said that George Washington stayed there before crossing the Delaware during the Revolutionary War. Gigi said that if the father of our country could cross the river and survive, so could she. She was determined to finish the transition.

First, Gigi and Tom went to New Hope for an initial consultation with Dr. McGinn. She examined Gigi, reviewed the referral letters and explained the surgery. Dr. McGinn had undergone the MTF surgery herself in 2000, and was previously known as Christopher. She is a strong woman who made it through the surgery. She is a plastic surgeon. Shortly, after her surgery, she started the Papillon Center as a referral and support agency for those undergoing the procedure. She did this when she realized that generally there is no counseling or assistance available pre- or post-op. She began performing the surgeries herself in 2005. One of the things that she emphasized during the visits was that this was serious surgery and that Gigi could die. While the statement was very sobering, Gigi still wanted to go ahead. She believed this was where life had been leading her since she was a child, and she was going to follow her path no matter where it took her.

The surgery was scheduled for mid-November 2013. The week before was crazy. Tom and Gigi were closing the salon for two weeks, so both were working to see as many of their regular customers as they could. Many brought gifts and wished them well. There was a lot of attention and a lot of discussion about the surgery. By the end of the week, Gigi was exhausted when she went to the bank and the manager and all the staff made a fuss over her. Suddenly, she was having a panic attack. She couldn't breathe or focus on her surroundings. Sweating and in a panic, she ran out of the bank. It took her some time to get it under control, but she did. Gigi was pretty shaken and wanted to leave the salon which was full of customers. Tom told her they couldn't and they stayed. Little attention was paid to her or her fears. Everyone was so busy congratulating her that no one saw the state she was in or the level of anxiety that was just under the surface.

On the following Sunday afternoon they drove to New Hope. Gigi took all of her panic and anxiety with her and no matter what she did, the thoughts didn't go away. When they arrived, there were several tests and blood work and she was told that her iron levels were low and that she might have to have a blood transfusion before surgery. The panic increased. By the time they arrived at the inn where they were spending the night, she was so nervous about the surgery and possible transfusion that she was pacing and talking a mile a minute. Her mind took off, and she was suddenly repeatedly going through all the worst outcomes. Her mind wouldn't stop and she had a severe panic attack and just had to get out of there. She begged Tom to take her home, and after talking with the doctor, he did. She thought, "So I have a penis; many transgender individuals do". For the next few days, she said that the surgery wasn't going to change her in any way that mattered. She'd keep her body the way God created it.

When they got home, they re-opened the salon and continued life as usual. For the first time, she was ambivalent about the process. The physicians and counselor all agreed that she should have been on a mild tranquilizer before the surgery. All the fuss over the procedure did not help. After a few weeks, she realized that she had no choice but to try again. It was still her dream and she was willing to take the leap. After a lot of soul searching and discussions with Tom, they decided together to reschedule the surgery for the beginning of January 2014 when Dr. McGinn had a cancellation.

The holidays passed and the surgery date was rapidly approaching. Everyone didn't make such a fuss this time. She got to New Hope in good shape and had the surgery the next morning without any problems. The average MTF surgery takes three to five hours; Gigi's took a little over four. For the following three days, she had to lay perfectly still in bed. After that, everything went fine. Within a few days she was up walking the corridors, talking and joking with everyone. Then, one night Tom took her for a walk around the corridors and she became so fatigued that she went to bed right away and fell to sleep. She woke up a few hours later screaming. She was seeing things, thinking she was home and talking to people who weren't there. They sedated her and transferred her to the ICU. Tom spent the night in the ICU wondering whether she was going to live or die. In moments when consciousness returned, Gigi thought that surely she was going to die right then.

The medical staff never did figure out what happened but thought she might have had a reaction to the many drugs she was on. Whether it was one drug or the mixture of cocktails, they didn't know what happened and had no way of finding out. For almost a week, she was pretty out of it and almost comatose. Tom sat vigil at the hospital night and day. He would walk the corridors for exercise and was amazed at the number of people facing the procedure and complications by themselves. These souls are especially brave, facing such a difficult time all alone. So at night, Tom would quietly walk the ward and visit with them. He was especially touched by one patient who did have his mother at his side. The mother's family had broken all contact with her because of her son's surgery. But his mother stayed, holding his hand. And, as a result, she lost her marriage and her other children. Tom said there was no bitterness in her, just love and support for her son. She sat vigil and held his hand as Tom did for Gigi.

Slowly, Gigi improved. She learned how to control the new bladder structure and continuously iced the new vagina. She also started dilating the vagina, a process that continues for a year. This is to ensure that the new organ stays open. At first, this hurts; then there is no feeling, and finally sensation is normal. The medical professionals involve the patient's partner in the process and teach them what to do. Tom was ready to assist when Gigi was released and prepared to help her in any way he could.

When they released Gigi from the hospital, she was supposed to go to a local cottage for two weeks to stay close to the hospital in case of further complications. She was so agitated that she refused and she insisted on going straight home. She still thought she was going to die and go to hell at any moment. They gave her extra medications to make the three hour ride home more comfortable. The meds also made her very argumentative and more than a tad depressed. On the drive home, they stopped at a rest stop. Tom went in to get some snacks and to get away from Gigi for a few minutes. She was driving him crazy. While he was gone, someone knocked on the window and asked Gigi if she could move the car to make room for him. Always agreeable, she pulled out her keys and said sure, and promptly backed the car into a tree. Poor Tom had such trouble explaining this to the police and insurance company. But, he finally managed and they called a friend to come from upstate New York to New Jersey to get them. It made the trip home unbearable.

The first weeks home were terrible. The penis that was no longer there hurt like crazy and Gigi was sure it was still there. Phantom pains were explained to her several times to no avail. She was weak and tired, and just walking about the house exhausted her. She was depressed and in a state that she had never experienced before. When you give serious drugs to a former addict, brain chemicals that have been dormant for years come to life again. She cried (like sitting in the corner sobbing and screaming) and went through horrible withdrawal again. Either she didn't want to get out of bed or continuously and quickly paced around the house. This was like the weeks in the rehab program but so much worse. And, she had such remorse about the whole thing. She felt that God had made her a man and she would be eternally damned for changing that. Tom finally arranged for a priest to come to the house. He sat on the floor and talked to her for hours. This holy man made her realize that God loves his children no matter what. She hadn't been very religious in years but a wonderful outcome of this awful time was that she found her way back to God and thanked God and the Virgin Mary for getting her through.

As time went on, being closed up was driving Gigi crazy. One day, Tom called her cousin and asked her to visit and take Gigi to the salon for a little bit. They couldn't get the garage door opener to work and kept trying to run under the door as it closed. This had no success. Then, they locked themselves in the backyard and it took 15 minutes to figure out that Gigi had a key to the back door in her pocket. They even tried to climb their fairly high white picket fence. They ended up sitting in snow, laughing and crying and couldn't stop. When Tom heard the story, he said they were like Lucy and Ethel. For Gigi, it was a good day and experience. She was out and laughing for the first time in weeks. She slowly realized that she was alive and was going to make it. But, it was a slow and difficult process that took so much, physically and emotionally, out of her.

A NEW WOMAN

She looked the same and acted the same. But, she let everyone know she wasn't the same. Gigi was well and happier than ever. She was finally okay with herself and didn't have any desire for anything else. Well, maybe bigger breasts. She kept looking at magazines for new ones. Tom didn't leave her and their relationship and sex life adapted easily to Gigi's new gender. They fumbled through and learned how to relate to each other again, like it was the beginning. It was like their relationship was new and they were rediscovering each other.

Soon after, Tom asked Gigi to marry him. Of course, she said yes. People asked all sorts of strange questions about the big change and they just calmly answered them. Their favorites were the ones asking whether they were both heterosexual all along. They would say that others were over-thinking and analyzing the situation. They were who they always said they were: two people in love with each other. She was the wife and Tom was the husband. But, they had unique ties to and understanding of the gay and transgender worlds. Other than the few horrible weeks post-surgery, Gigi didn't regret the surgery at all. Everything felt right. It was how things were supposed to be.

This said, you should not get the impression that it was an easy transition and that it fixed all of Gigi's problems. The suicide rate of MTF surgery patients is high: twenty percent higher than the average. People think the surgery will solve everything wrong in their lives. It doesn't. If you were prone to depression and anxiety, you still will be after your surgery. If you go in a sad miserable person, chances are that you will come out that way. For Gigi, after she healed, it made her feel whole physically and mentally. The dose of estrogen was decreased and all the meds she took in preparation for the surgery were stopped. However, she still had some anxiety and depression. But, it was so much less than before. And, some things went full circle. The boy (now man) who assaulted her with the dance trophy years ago called to apologize. He said his son is gay and that he has learned how difficult the life can be and that he was sorry he was so terrible to her when they were young. He admitted that he tormented her because of her gender identification. He was ashamed and said he had learned the gift of acceptance and understood the issue much better after dealing with it more closely.

Her favorite story is from a day shortly after the surgery when her sister came into the salon. Mary came in and said in a loud, confident voice, "So, where is my little sister?" Her sister was there. She had fully transitioned from George to Gigi. And, she loved it. She was still taking voice lessons and they were back to a regular routine and the business was thriving. Were there times when she wished she didn't do it? You bet. The surgery and the pain afterwards were awful, emotionally and physically. But, now, she thought she faced the rest of her life as the person she was always meant to be. And, Tom was still by her side and largely responsible for her still being here.

After 37 years together, Thomas Rosselli and Gigi Catherine Conboy were married on May 17, 2015 at a ceremony at the Gideon Putnam Hotel in Saratoga Springs.

They were surrounded by 70 family and friends and lots of love to begin their new adventure. The sun was out and the state park adjacent to the hotel was gorgeous. Gay marriage had been legal in New York State since 2011, but, Gigi didn't want to get married until she felt whole and was who she was supposed to be. She also thought that Tom wanted to wait until they could marry in the Catholic Church. A friend of theirs filed online for a minister's license and performed the May ceremony. But, by now, both also wanted a ceremony in the Catholic Church. So, after the first ceremony, they resumed their efforts to get Church approval and started counseling with a few priests. The end result was a second ceremony on August 3, 2015. This event could probably be a story by itself. The internet says that there are records of some marriages in the Church of couples who have had transition surgery. Gigi and Tom were one of those couples. The second wedding in a Catholic Church was small and intimate, and very touching. Afterwards, Gigi would tell everyone that she was really married and had two weddings to make sure the first one took.

After the Church ceremony, Gigi and Tom knelt in front of the Blessed Virgin's statue and thanked her for helping them to get to this point. They both looked so serene. At their home, the few guests stood in the kitchen or sat around the pool and talked about their lives and the difficult path they had traveled. Everyone thought that it would be happily ever after for Mr. and Mrs. Rosselli. This was not to be.

Wedding 1

Wedding 2

CHAOS EVER AFTER

Up to here. Gigi's story was written about three years ago. After their wedding ceremonies, Gigi and Tom seemed to be having their "happily ever after" or, at least that is what everyone hoped. Gigi went on a spending spree to end all sprees. Weekends, the couple would roam the streets of Saratoga and she would buy whatever struck her fancy. The sales clerks at all the stores knew her. It was kind of like "Hello Dolly", with word spreading quickly that Gigi was in town. Tom was exceedingly generous, buying her all sorts of jewelry. The collection expanded weekly and was shown to all in the salon. Gigi had waited all her life to be a woman and she was enjoying every minute of it.

After a few months, though, things seemed to change. At first, they were small changes. But, most of their customers and friends only saw them a few times a month. Some changes quickly accelerated. First, Gigi began to lose focus very easily. She would be doing hair and stop repeatedly to have extended conversations with everyone in the salon and everyone who came in, like the mailman and the UPS and the FedEx drivers. She would also stop and talk to everyone that called or walked by. Customers would say "Gigi, my hair" and she would refocus for a few minutes. She seemed to be increasingly dependent on Tom to mix colors, find her scissors and tell her who was next and what treatment they were having. Sometimes she didn't show for appointments because she had a headache. She also lost all interest in this book and completing it. It was more a short story than a book, but it was almost done. It just needed a conclusion and some photos to complement the narrative. She would put it off repeatedly and then finally said she was in no hurry to complete it. Before this, it had been a priority. Then, out of the blue, she would ask why it wasn't finished. She had no memory of not wanting to finish it and insisted it wasn't so.

We lost contact for a while and I didn't see her for a few months. Actually, we were angry at each other but pretending not to be. I was mad about the confusion over the book and the hours it took to get my hair done. She was mad that I was mad, and that I went somewhere else to get a haircut. Finally, I stopped in the salon to say hello and was stunned by the change. I had the parts of the story that we had finished printed and offered it to her as a peace offering. She gleefully accepted it and told me my hair looked nice. I knew she didn't mean it. And we both laughed.

Gigi recognized people right away but their conversations were bizarre. She pulled friends and family aside to talk about Tom. She said she was upset that "this man (Tom) had keys to her salon and home" and would ask you to get them back. Everyone said that Tom was her husband and she would say of course he was. But, a few minutes later, she would repeat the conversation. A few weeks later, she started saying that she wanted to divorce Tom and let him live his own life. She felt she was too old for him and didn't want to hold him back. Then, she would answer the phone and yell at callers saying that she didn't want to deal with them anymore. You could see and feel her frustration. She was lost. A customer came in and she chased her out and into the parking lot. She pulled the hairdryer off another customer who thought Gigi was going to attack her. Tom didn't know what to do. She was destroying their business and just wanted to shop and spend lots of money. He feared she was developing early onset dementia, since dementia and mental health issues ran in her family. He readily admitted that their life was a mess and that he was having difficulty getting her to see doctors to find out what was wrong.

Close family had one more contact with Gigi before a diagnosis was received. It was also strange. Usually, when they called, Tom would be on the line and say, "Hi, it's Gigi and Tom" and they would have a three way conversation. Well, one Saturday afternoon in the early winter of 2017, Gigi called close family by herself and asked everyone to make sure that someone would take care of Tom. It was snowing and all of their customers canceled so they were at home. She said she knew she was seriously ill and didn't know what was happening, but she wanted to make sure that Tom was okay without her. She didn't explain more, that was it. Everyone agreed to do what she asked. She then hung up and the line went dead. She knew the end was coming and was worried about Tom's well-being without her.

TOM'S STORY

The rest of the story was written from Tom's perspective and after Gigi became ill. There is some repetition, but it is necessary. It is the same story from someone else's eyes. Tom gave me more detail than Gigi and over time he would remember additional events to add. So, we start by going back to the Italian family from Albany with whom Gigi found a home.

If ever there was an unlikely couple, it was George Conboy and Thomas Rosselli. They met on August 5, 1977 at a gay bar in Albany. George was nine years older than Tom. And, although George was four years out of rehab, he was still struggling with his sobriety; he was quite drunk the night they met. Tom was entering his senior year of high school at Bishop McGinn, an officer of his class and halfway through the cosmetology program at Austin Beauty School in Albany. Tom did not drink or smoke and had no desire to do so. He didn't know he was gay and had never even thought about it. For every sad memory Gigi had, Tom had a wonderful memory. Tom's main interest was music and that was why he sneaked into the Eight Ball Club that night. His hero was John Travolta and his favorite movie "Saturday Night Fever". He tried to dress and act like Travolta and had a real style going on. He was glued to American Bandstand most afternoons and was a real fan of Soul Train. He was loved and cared for at home and was just happy being who he was. That night, he wanted to listen to the music and be left alone. He wasn't looking for company, either male or female.

Tom Rosselli was born October 10, 1959 to Josephine DeNigiris and Joseph Rosselli, both first generation Italian-Americans. Josephine's family came from the Foggia region in Northern Italy and Joseph's from a small island off the coast of Capri. Josephine's father, Michael DeNigris, had become a barber because his mother had told him it was a respectable "white collar" job. And, he always did what his mother told him to do. When he fell in love with a German girl, his mother found him a respectable Italian girl to marry instead, and married they stayed. Michael (Tom's grandfather) always told Tom that "in the old country" their family made barrels for wine and vinegar. This was also a very honorable profession. Tom's parents, Josephine and Joseph, met in New York City, and after their marriage moved to Albany along with their entire families. Tom's grandfather opened a barbershop and his uncle later opened a beauty salon.

Joseph Rosselli was a machinist at the Watervliet Arsenal. He left for work every morning just before 6 AM and returned precisely at 4:15 PM. He took a five minute shower and then sat at the dining room table with a drink and the mail. Tom's aunts who lived in the second and third floor apartments got home at five and the entire family ate dinner together at 5:15 PM. Dinner took a while with everyone talking at the same time. This kind of routine made everyone feel secure and added to the happiness of the home. Tom can't imagine growing up any other way. The Rossellis had four children, Sal, Barbara, Tom and Mary Jo. Sal was 11 years older than Tom and Barbara was 10 years older; Mary Jo was two years younger. Sal and Barbara were like an extra set of loving parents for Tom and

Mary Jo. Sal was valedictorian of his high school class and Barbara was very beautiful and stylish. Tom still remembers the way she did her eyes, so glamorous. There were also grandparents, aunts and uncles and cousins that lived in their house and neighborhood. Mary Jo died in 2000 of cancer and Tom and Barbara helped to take care of her during the last years of her life. Love and caring was all around and she died peacefully at the age of 38. Sal now lives in California and Barbara lives not far from Tom. The three of them are all still very close.

Tom's family lived in Albany, first at 113 Grand Street and then moving uptown to 11 A Woodlawn Avenue. The first neighborhood was very Italian, and also ethnically diverse. The second neighborhood was very Jewish. One of the older ladies on his block taught Tom Yiddish. To this day, Tom speaks it fairly well. His earliest memories are of snowy nights on Grand Street when the family would sit around and talk and just watch the snow. Then, they would collect snow and his aunt would use coffee and sugar to make Italian ice for all of them. He remembers all the religious holidays and the family going to church all together. He felt the serenity of the holidays and love at home and church. Another favorite day for him was the first day of school. He viewed each year as a new beginning, a chance to get to know everyone again and enjoy the community of the school yard. His mother was the center of his childhood and of the neighborhood. She helped everybody. Tom remembers when the mother of a neighbor was dying at home. Josephine brought the neighbor's seven children to the Rosselli house to sleep on blankets on the floor in the living room. Josephine thought the children were too young to witness death. Her door was always open and the inn was always full.

Some of Tom's friends thought he might be gay. So, on that August night in 1977, they took him to two straight clubs and one gay club. Since he wasn't 18, they got him in by lying about his age. There he was at the Eight Ball Club sitting by himself when a drunk George Conboy came up to him and tried to get him a drink or cigarette. When neither approach worked, they started talking and they talked for a long while. Neither expected what the future would hold. Finally about 2 AM, Tom's friends came and told him they had to leave. Outside, they warned Tom about George advising him to stay away.

Tom quietly listened to his friends all the way home, then went inside, took his mother's keys and drove back to the Eight Ball Club. George and he spoke for three more hours. Tom wasn't thinking about being gay or straight. He simply saw a person he wanted to be with. He says that he knew right away he and George would be life partners. About 5:30 that morning George asked Tom if he had a car to drive George back to Cohoes. At 17, Tom could only think that his mother would kill him if he left Albany. So, he said no. He then waited until George left with someone else and went home himself. The next day he returned to the club and asked the bartender how to contact George. He told him, and they met a few days after and kept seeing each other. They quickly became a couple and that was that.

Over the next month, Tom and George got to know each other. Tom introduced George to his parents as his new friend from Cohoes. Tom's mother was startled at this; the only thing she knew about Cohoes was that it was the name of a clothing outlet where the neighbors bought their clothes. Tom had a difficult time explaining that there was a town around the store and, no, George was not homeless and did not live in a department store.

Tom had always been truthful with his parents and this "friend" thing seemed deceptive. So, on Labor Day weekend, not even a month after they met, he came clean with his parents and told them that he and George were a couple. His parents supported him in his choice. Imagine this, it is 1977 and you find out your 17-year-old son is gay. Your entire family is very religious, with the usual morals and values of the time. You are even old world conservative. But, you don't blink an eye and welcome his partner into the family with open arms. This was remarkable. This was the Rossellis.

The acceptance was not universal. Tom's aunts were very judgmental toward George. He was not only gay, but came from a poor family that was frequently on welfare. In this Italian family this was worse than being gay. His brother heard the stories about substance abuse and crossdressing and thought Tom should walk away. The aunts wanted to send him away to be cured or to become a priest. Tom had the maturity to ignore his loved ones and just chuckled. George started coming to the family dinners and over time was accepted by almost everyone.

After Tom finished high school, he moved in with George. At first, the new couple lived in George's apartment on Remsen Street and then moved to an apartment complex on the Cohoes hill. For a short time, both worked at salons in malls. George did a lot of studying to learn about credit and financing and soon they opened their own business on Fulton Street in Troy. It wasn't long after that they purchased a trailer and moved to Halfmoon. So now they had their own business and home. And, there was so much more to come. Tom says that Gigi never said the words "I am a woman" to him early in the relationship. George told him that he preferred dressing as a woman and loved female clothes. George was very feminine acting in his movements. Over the next few years, Tom figured out on his own that George wanted to transition and they slowly started to talk about it.

Neither Tom nor George came from money. George's family was frequently on public assistance and Tom's family struggled to remain self-sufficient. Everything the couple built was a result of their own efforts. Over the years, they would move from the trailer to a home on the hill in Waterford, to another one off of Route 9 in Colonie, and finally to a home in Loudonville. George furnished each with love and care. Each home was a true reflection of their personalities. Tom loved to swim and behind each home George had a swimming pool installed. In Loudonville, George even had a fountain installed in the pool because Tom likes to swim in the rain. Tom did the landscaping and discovered he had a green thumb. The homes were beautiful and tributes to each of them. They also moved their business to a location just outside of Cohoes. And, their client base continued to grow. They were successful and happy in their relationship and at work.

Did George stop drinking right away? No. But over time, he did. Especially after they opened their own salon, he avoided alcohol. In later years, Gigi would occasionally have a Grey Goose and Cranberry juice. But, it was very rare. It was just another part of her life that she controlled. George had always wanted to transition. Tom knew this and was not opposed and supported him through the minor surgeries. George became Gigi and again Tom was supportive. He describes Gigi as always being girly and gorgeous. She was glamorous like his sister and loved dressing up on long weekends in New York City. When they would go to "The Night of a 100 Gowns", she would dress up and entertain. She also loved to shop but Tom describes early sprees as reasonable. Later, after the full transition, the spending became out of line. But, he indulged her knowing that she waited all her life to become a girl. Tom admits that when she started talking about the transition surgery, he was concerned. Not because he didn't want her to do it; it was because of the risk to her health and life. When he heard Dr. McGinn describe the surgery, he would have been happy if she changed her mind. But, she didn't. So forward they went.

Tom and Gigi argued but never thought about breaking up. Their discussions about the transition were no different. Tom supported her. Her cancelling the first time was okay with him. Her almost dying the second time was not. Tom's faith got him through though. For Tom, faith is the center of his life. As the son of such a devout Italian family, it was bound to be strong. But because of his parents and teachers, the church and his beliefs were very real to him. He says that no matter how much he loved his parents and family, and loves Gigi, he always loves God first and trusts God to do what is best for him. He sat and prayed by Gigi's bedside at New Hope and knew she would recover. He didn't panic or despair. He just knew. What did worry him was the possibility of complications after the surgery and what the long-term effects would be.

After the surgery, everything happened so quickly it was a blur to Tom. He quickly re-opened the salon and took care of all of their customers. Gigi had a crisis of faith; Tom found a priest to come to the house and help her find God again. Tom spoiled her even more and indulged her desire for expensive clothes and jewelry. He felt she had waited so long to be a woman that she deserved everything she wanted and he got it for her. He realizes now that he spoiled her rotten and that they went overboard: he is not sorry at all. Her new wardrobe was mostly from Lily Pulitzer, Chico's and Macy's; everything fit to perfection. Tom says that even before she transitioned Gigi never looked like she was in "drag". Everything had to be as real as possible. After the surgery, she wasn't completely satisfied with her new breast size. It had increased to 36 B from the hormones; Gigi felt because of her height and other measurements "they" should have been larger. Tom thinks that they would have been if she didn't become ill. But he also feels at 5'9" and 138 pounds she was perfect.

The most frequently asked question before and after the surgery was what happens when one member of a gay couple transitions to another sex. Tom feels that this is just silly. His relationship with Gigi was never based on sexual identities. It was two souls and hearts who found each other and were meant to join. Their sex life was different but still good. After the surgery, Tom helped Gigi dilate at night and would massage her feet and legs that were so tired and achy as she recuperated. They would spend this time talking and renewing their changed relationship. Some mornings as Gigi came out of the shower Tom said he would just think how gorgeous she was and how grateful he was for their relationship. She was and is his perfect partner and he was happy. He says that he never looked at another man or woman this way. It was and always will be Gigi.

Soon, Tom proposed and Gigi accepted. They had always planned on marrying and the time seemed right. He proposed in Chianti, a fancy restaurant in Saratoga. He would have preferred to do it when they were alone, but Gigi liked an audience. He told her that it was time for them to wed, that she was his life and would always be the center of his universe. She cried, giggled and said yes. The restaurant patrons clapped. Afterwards, they went to her favorite jeweler and picked out a ring and then went to her favorite stores to tell everyone. They planned a ceremony in Saratoga with a friend officiating and about 70 friends and family present. Gigi had three dresses and changed after the ceremony and once in the middle of the reception. They were all short cocktail dresses and all were beautiful. She walked down the aisle to "There She Is, Miss America" and she sang her favorite songs during the reception. In August, there was a second ceremony in the Church. Tom had an angelic smile all day. For this private ceremony, Gigi had a dress designed and made for her by a local designer; it was white lace with a handkerchief hemline. Again, it was gorgeous. Tom remembers Gigi as always being "girly-girly" and feminine. Her new body just made her more so. And, now, she loved showing off her new lace underwear and would invite half of the Macy's staff in the dressing room with her to choose new underwear and ask if they thought her breasts were big enough.

THE DISEASE

They were happier than ever and things seemed to be going well. But, Tom had started noticing some small changes even before their weddings. Gigi was frequently overwhelmed and saying things like "How are we going to get this all done?" Before, she had believed that they could get anything and everything done together. She couldn't keep her appointments straight and Tom took over all of the scheduling. Still, they had some wonderful times, afternoons in Saratoga and dinners at local restaurants. Some nights, they would ride back from Saratoga singing Broadway songs and enjoying sunsets over Saratoga Lake. They danced at concerts in Green Island with Annie Lazzaro and laughed a lot. They had waited so long to have their "happily ever after" and loved every moment of it.

That Christmas, Gigi told friends and family that they were having an open house on a Sunday in December. When no one heard anything from her, they called to find out the time. She simply said she had forgotten all about it and had made no preparations. It seemed so strange and so did how she acted in the salon. This behavior progressed as they went into 2016. Tom went all out that Christmas. He put up five indoor trees and decorated all the evergreen trees in the yard with white lights. Gigi would stand and watch the wonderland outside and ooh and ahh over the beautiful setting. She told Tom it was the best Christmas ever.

Gigi was always driven, her mind always going. She was aware of her family background and was determined that she wouldn't and couldn't be like her parents. She was going to be successful and stay successful. Now, whatever was going on in her head seemed too much for her. She would zone out and become quiet or argumentative. It started being like it was when she would go into the Cohoes Library drunk, only worse, a lot worse.

2016 was not a good year. Tom was more and more aware that something was seriously wrong. Gigi only wanted to shop and go to Saratoga. She would almost push customers out of the salon to do so. Tom learned that if Gigi took a long break in the middle of the day, they could sometimes extend their work day and continue to operate the business. Tom said that he will always cherish the conversations they had on the rides, about everything and anything. They talked a lot about Gigi's illness, but also discussed almost everything else. Holding hands on the ride back, he would try to coax her into going back to the salon. But, very quickly, she started to refuse and insisted on going home.

Soon, Gigi didn't want to work at all and Tom kept trying to keep their business going. At night, they would cuddle on the sofa and Gigi would ask Tom if everything would be okay. He told her he didn't know but was worried, and they would both cry and hold onto each other. They went to doctors looking for answers: first, there was blood work, an endocrinologist and routine physicals. No one found anything wrong. The consensus was that the problems were caused by hormone changes after the surgery. They suggested an MRI but Gigi avoided that. She didn't want to look for more trouble that she knew was there.

By the summer, Gigi couldn't style or cut hair at all and instead would shampoo customers, apply color applications and roll hair for customers who still used rollers. Every so often she would get so frustrated and angry that she would throw things and scream at customers to get out. Tom would do everything else while trying to keep Gigi calm and focused on the tasks at hand. It was difficult and then became impossible. She also became very territorial, telling everyone that the salon and home were hers. It seemed like if she couldn't control her actions she wanted to control her things. She would tell Tom that the salon was hers, and that he should start his own business. He would tell her that he would leave but that he would take his customers with him. She would then tell him to stay. She would want his keys from the house and salon, and he would give them to her. Of course, he had others. If Tom fought with her, she would get more defensive. So, he would just go along and seemingly agree with her. He knew that many customers wanted him to intervene and control her behavior but he didn't want to exacerbate her actions. She was his wife first and business partner second. He wanted to care for Gigi more than save the business. This left the business really struggling.

THE DIAGNOSIS

In early November, 2016, Gigi walked out of the salon for the last time as owner and lead stylist. She needed to stay home and have 24-hour care. She felt safe with Tom and at home. She wanted to avoid all other situations. The salon's hours were reduced and Tom struggled to continue caring for his regular customers. He would meet clients at the salon at night, leaving Gigi asleep at home. He would also hire friends and family to stay with her. He even did hair in their garage on a few nights. Gigi would react to Tom in two different ways, first, as a safety zone and caretaker and also as a target of her anger and frustrations. She postponed the MRI to February of 2017 and soon after received the diagnosis of Frontal Temporal Dementia (FTD). Tom, Gigi and Gigi's niece, Mary Ellen, sat in the physician's office listening to the prognosis. Words such as terminal and three to five years hung in the air. During this period, Gigi's frontal lobe would either slowly or quickly disintegrate and she would lose the ability to talk, walk and eat. Medications were prescribed to make her comfortable. No cure or treatment was available. It was TERMINAL. They all just stared into space in their own worlds.

DEVASTATION

Life as Gigi and Tom knew it was over. One of Gigi's friends had died of the disease a few years before. This was Debbie Dumas who used to cut school with her when they were teenagers. When Gigi learned that Debbie was sick and later that she died, Gigi sat down and cried. This was before her own diagnosis. But she remembered Debbie well and said she had always been so nice to her.

Tom describes the disease well. He tells you that Alzheimer's is a memory impairment umbrella under which many specific dementias fall, including FTD. FTD is one of the worst medically and fiscally. It is definitely the most expensive disease. Frequently, FTD starts with a head trauma; this was not the case for Gigi. This is followed by many symptoms, including an overwhelmed feeling, the deletion of memories and mania. The intensity of the symptoms will vary from patient to patient. The prognosis is the same. It can be mistaken for Parkinson's or ALS. With Gigi they nailed the diagnosis right after the MRI. Medical professionals also assured them that there was no connection between the transition surgery and the FTD diagnosis. Many family and friends didn't believe this. But all research says that the two are not connected.

In the month following the diagnosis, Gigi started to have severe manic symptoms. She wanted to jump through windows and drive her car off the road. Tom quickly disposed of the car. He couldn't soothe her or reassure her enough, and really couldn't leave her. His plan was that when he felt she could hurt herself or others, he would take her to the hospital. The first time came in April. Albany Medical Center tried to find some medications that would keep her mood stable and her body functioning. At the hospital, her preoccupation was going home and getting out of the locked unit. She wanted to go back to her safe zone, home. After ten days, they released her. Her niece Mary Ellen stayed with her when Tom couldn't be there. During this time, the family had some good times. They celebrated Gigi's birthday on April 5. Mary Ellen and Gigi became extremely close. Tom would come home and find them huddled in conversation about all things or asleep in each other's arms on the sofa. Some nights, Gigi and Tom would dance to music that they loved and it seemed that she was okay. Tom always knew that the need for 24 hour facility care was near. Gigi would look at their wedding photos and identify every person in each picture. Mary Ellen would read the finished sections of this book to her and she would talk about each experience remembering all the details. It was at this point that Tom decided to finish the book as a tribute to her. The project began once again.

A second hospitalization came in early June. This time, Gigi was at Albany Medical Center for a few days before they arranged to transfer her to the Memory Care Unit of a local nursing home. Gigi went in on a Thursday and left the following Thursday. During that time, she was constantly manic and wanting "out". Several of her friends and nieces visited. She knew everyone and introduced them correctly to others. With me, she suggested we go for a "walk" and I agreed. There was a fenced area almost all the way around the home and soon we were "walking". Gigi was actually running. I am over a half foot shorter, had heels on and was carrying my pocketbook. I couldn't keep up and was trailing behind. When we would get to the end of the fenced in area, she would want to climb over the fence. I said we couldn't do that and she responded with "It's not like we haven't done it before! Let's get out of here." She was referring to the time we locked ourselves in her backyard and tried to scale their fence. She obviously remembered this well.

Again, she was only interested in escape. When I was ready to leave, I made the mistake of telling her so. She panicked and wanted me to take her with me. The aides had to pull her off me. Medical professionals called this redirecting. I called it bodily force. Tom would visit Gigi each night and hold her while she went to sleep. When Mary Ellen visited, she would tell her she was going to the restroom when leaving. Smart!! On the next Thursday, another niece visited and did what I did when leaving. "Bye, Aunt Gigi, I am leaving now." All hell broke loose. Two aides tried to "redirect" her attention and this time Gigi was ready for them. She pushed the aides off of her and one fell backwards onto the floor. The police were called and Gigi was transported to yet another hospital. She was only there one night due to the good judgement of one of her physicians. This doctor thought, "My God, this woman has been in four places in the last week; we need to get her settled". They moved her to a secure, private-pay facility where she lived from June 2017 until February 2018.

In her new home, the change was dramatic. She had difficulty holding her head up and shuffled when she walked. Her room overlooked the entrance and when she recognized her visitors she would welcome them in a loud voice. When the door was closed, it locked behind you. It was scary for visitors, but most of all for her. She needed assistance eating and had difficulty swallowing and ate so very little. There were cameras in each room that monitored each patient and their every move. She spoke a lot and repeatedly would say "it" (FTD) could happen to anyone. She knew the doctors had told her this.

Gigi was in this home until February of 2018. Tom had been looking for another facility for some time: he found a small private care facility in the country. He packed her clothes in the car the night of February 13th and was scheduled to transfer her himself the following morning. He was really not satisfied with the care provided. The facility was supposed to provide one on one care but didn't and Gigi spent a lot of time locked in her room. Also, at the new home, she could wear her own clothes and sit outside when she wanted. At the first facility, she wore an institutional jumpsuit and was locked in. Before he picked her up on February 14, he received a call from the facility and was told that Gigi fell in her room and seemed to be seriously hurt. He told them to take her to Albany Medical Center where he met the ambulance. They soon found out that her right hip was broken. Up to this point, Gigi could walk long distances and talked constantly even if it didn't always make sense. This was all about to change.

Once in the hospital, the diagnosis of a broken hip was confirmed. The first night she was sedated while they used an imaging machine to place the hip back together. Two days later, surgery was performed to place pins in the broken hip. It was painful. Gigi was placed in a private room as is the policy for transgender patients. When visitors arrived, she recognized them and immediately said "Thank God you're here. Let's get out of here and go party somewhere, anywhere." She talked continuously but didn't really make much sense, other than expressing her intense wish to escape. About a week later, she was transferred to a skilled nursing facility for rehabilitation.

The repair of the broken hip was successful but the process intensified the FTD. Soon, Gigi could hardly talk, except an occasional few words to Tom. One of the last things she said was to tell him to take care of himself. The love still flowed between them. She spent most of her time in bed and was frequently curled in a fetal position. There was no effort to get her on her feet again. Her hands and arms would shake, sometimes violently. During this time, Tom was given a little dog that would bring smiles to her face. The dog was called "Little Gigi". Someone played the song "Cabaret" for her and she shed some tears. Friends and family would talk to her and sit and hold her hand, and sing songs. When asked if she could talk, she would try but only random sounds came out. You knew by watching her eyes that she understood and that she was still there. She would smile and laugh with her eyes.

Gigi on her birthday in April 2017.
This would be her last birthday at home.

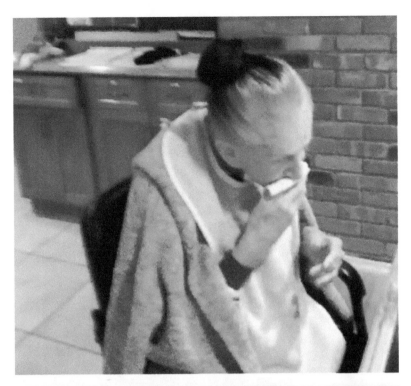

(ABOVE AND TOP OF NEXT PAGE) Pictures of Gigi in the Adult Home where she lived from August 2017 to January 2018.

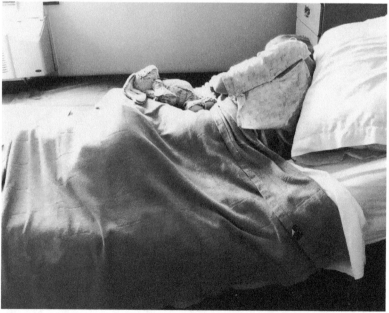

Gigi at the last nursing home just a few weeks before her death.

THE COMING OF THE SOUL

Frontal Temporal Dementia is usually diagnosed in individuals in their late 50s or early 60s. Gigi was 66 when she received the diagnosis. It is a rare form of dementia. The patient shows a gradual, progressive decline in behavior and language. Their memory is usually preserved. They are still there, but locked inside a withering body and brain. As the disease progresses, the patient becomes completely dependent on caregivers.

For over a full year after Gigi's diagnosis, she required 24-hour care. Most likely, she had symptoms of FTD several years before. Little things that everyone thought were quirky were actually signs of what was to come. It was difficult to tell since Gigi never had any boundaries and regularly did outrageous things. In the first facility, she would fall to sleep repeating the Serenity prayer. She remembered it word for word and said it over and over. But, way too soon, she could not talk and had difficulty eating.

For the first year that Gigi was in a facility, Tom went to mass every morning, then to work and finally to see Gigi. This was his life. Throughout, he remained focused on the task at hand and had faith that all will be well. But, everyone knew the eventual outcome. Gigi who was so full of life a few years ago had trouble walking. Gigi who loved eating decadently, delicious food had trouble swallowing. Gigi who had a zest for living and danced through each day could not move. Throughout it all, Tom sat with her.

Tom tried to find another placement for her, still wanting something a little more like home. But then in early May of 2018, she developed an infection and was treated with intravenous antibiotics. Soon, she needed oxygen and then required IV fluids. She was quickly unable to swallow and stopped eating. Gigi was placed in hospice on May 15 and died early in the morning of May 17, 2018 on their third wedding anniversary. Tom had spent the night with her and curled into bed with her. She relaxed, stopped shaking and straightened her legs. She died in his arms with a smile on her face. Mary Ellen had spent a good part of the night with them; but, Gigi waited until it was just her and Tom and gently went into the morning light.

At her wake, a few days later, the line went out to the street. Politicians, clients, friends and family said their final goodbyes. The next day, the priest told everyone a beautiful story about the soul and body. Gigi who now dwelt in her soul was at rest. She was taken to her final resting place with the bells of St. Mary's in downtown Albany ringing a final goodbye.

Having said all of this, you can hear Gigi saying, "Girlfriend that is just too sad. Life is not the end point; it is a journey. I lived fully and followed my dreams. I knew I was a woman and never pretended to be anyone else. I removed every barrier to finding my true self. I loved to entertain and did so every day in my salon. I loved life and just being with people made me happy. I found a love that many never dreamed of and loved "my Tommy" so. And, I will always hear the music and dance to its beat. I will always love you all."

WORDS FROM GIGI

Gigi was known for witty, pithy sayings; whatever you said she had a response. Here are a few examples:

This is a salon not a shop. You take your car to a shop. You take your hair to a salon. Remember this. It is important.

Use a shampoo that suds. It is better for your hair and it feels great when you massage it ever so slowly.

Be friendly to everyone: Talk to everyone you meet and always say something nice. Tell them that they have beautiful eyes, a beautiful outfit and gorgeous hair.

Always be polite: Smile at everyone. Gigi waved at passersby at the salon and cars that turned in front of her.

Spray your hair: mess it up and spray it again. Leave it that way. It looks better.

Tell everyone you love them. It helps the world be a nicer place. When you replied, I love you to, she would respond, and follow it up with I love you more.

Eat dessert first: you may not have room after dinner and it is a shame to miss the best part of the meal.

Dance every day. At outdoor concerts Gigi would go around and get the older men to dance with her. After a few minutes, she would ask their wives to dance with them and she would move on to another man.

Your hair looks like you did turns in the sheets. Was it fun? Details please--

O.M.G., you look like you are carved out of cream cheese. Yum.

No, we don't chop hair. We chop onions and meats. We style your hair and it will be beautiful. Trust me.

Chickens are plucked. We tweeze and shape your eyebrows. We don't pluck. If you want to pluck, get a chicken.

Gratuities are not expected but are always deeply appreciated.

It is not the big things that make us; it is the small things. Pay attention to them.

Why do you look so young? Please tell, who is the plastic surgeon?

You can never be too rich, too clean or too thin.

I was raised by "Mommy Dearest". It wasn't fun.

Are you religious? Do you have faith? I live with the Father, Son and Holy Ghost rolled into one! He is my moral compass. I would be lost without him.

ACKNOWLEDGMENTS

There are so many to thank for helping to make this book a reality. First and foremost are Gigi and Tom Rosseli. Gigi asked me to write this book and enthusiastically helped with the beginning sections. I am honored that she trusted me with her story. I enjoyed working with her and thank her for being so open and honest. I thank Tom for being brave enough to ask me to finish the book and for providing many more details to fill out the story. He also searched for the pictures and didn't complain once when I kept asking for more. They both were and are an important part of my life, teaching me so much about how to live well and fully.

There are my family and friends. They have put up with me talking about this book for four years. From the title to the words, they provided feedback and never told me to go away. Many friends and my niece, Danielle Berg provided editing help with early copies and encouragement to finish what I started. Special thanks to Pat Duchesne, Kathy Conboy Gillis, Shawna Lambert and Sheila Patterson for reading so many drafts and providing wonderful suggestions. I love you all.

Finally, sincere thanks to Carol DeMare and Jill Cooley for editing the final copies, and to to Jessika Hazelton from Troy Book Makers for her help in making the words and pictures into a book. All of your skills were amazing and you improved the work so much. Thank you, thank you, thank you.